SKATEBOARDING

SKATEBOARDING

by Dorothy Childers Schmitz

Library of Congress Catalog Card Number: 78-7048   Reprinted 1978

International Standard Book Numbers:
0-913940-91-7 Library Bound
0-89686-012-4

Edited by - Dr. Howard Schroeder
          Prof. in Reading and Language Arts
          Dept. of Elementary Education
          Mankato State University

Library of Congress
Cataloging in Publication Data

Schmitz, Dorothy Childers.
 Skateboarding

 (Funseekers)
 SUMMARY: Text and illustrations describe various types
of skateboards and skateboarding techniques.
  1. Skateboarding--Juvenile literature. (1.
Skateboards. 2. Skateboarding) I. Title
GV859.8.S35   796.2'1   78-7048
 ISBN 0-913940-91-7

   A special thanks to Jill Sherman, editor of Skateboard World Magazine.
An additional note of thanks goes out to photographer Stan Sharp, whose
photos strengthen the text of this book.

PHOTO CREDITS

Skateboard World Magazine, courtesy of Stan Sharp: Cover, 12, 13, 17, 19,
       21, 22, 25, 27, 28A, 28B, 29, 31, 32
Pete Hornby: 3, 8, 20, 24
Randal M. Heise: 5, 6
Mark E. Ahlstrom: 14A, 14B, 15, 16A, 16B

SKATEBOARDING

SKATEBOARDING

It's early morning — a crisp, autumn morning, perfect for downhilling. No one else is on the hill. You know that in less than an hour, the hill will be crowded. You've never done this hill before, so you measure it as you climb. You reach the top, take a last look down, mount and begin your descent. It feels right. You pick up speed, faster and faster. Maybe it's a little steeper than you thought. Better do a little traversing. Now a little wedeling. That's better. Even though you aren't half way down, you must be doing more than 30 MPH judging from the wind in your face, and the speed at which the trees race by on either side of the pavement. It's decision time. It's too late to butt-drag to a stop. You're going too fast for that. Do you ride it out or bail out? You check the traffic. No cars or pedestrians in sight, so you decide to ride it out. Bad decision. Nothing left to do but to step-off-the-nose-and-run. So you do just that. At the bottom at last, safely back on the grass, winded and a little shaken, you pick up your fiberglass that arrived just after you did. "Wow! That could have been a serious wipeout! Could have ruined my Saturday — several Saturdays! I'd better get in a little more flatland practice before I do this hill again."

What's it all about? Skateboarding! Ever since man invented the wheel, boys and girls have been finding ways to have fun with it. At this very moment, wheels are spinning across the land. Unicycles, bicycles, tricycles, scooters, wagons, and skateboards. Skateboarding is taking the country by storm. It became a big fad in the sixties, like the hula-hoop. But, unlike the hula-hoop, it didn't die. How many hula-hoops have you seen on the streets and sidewalks lately? Skateboards are everywhere!

Those boards of the sixties were primitive compared to the skateboards of today. Urethane has replaced the old clay wheels, and the old block-of-wood board may be anything from a plywood sandwich board, to aluminum, or fiberglass. The choices are endless, and your choice depends on how and where you're going to use it.

In many cities, you can find skateboard parks and arenas that have become the most popular places in town. People of all ages, shapes, and sizes are enjoying the sport, entering into competitions, or just having fun.

Some neighborhoods take care of their own skateboarders. They set aside times for certain streets to be closed to traffic so that skateboarders can enjoy the safety of their own quiet streets. Others have even drained swimming pools for skateboarding! But, wait! If you are just a beginner, you are not quite ready for that.

Choosing proper equipment is the first thing a beginner does. Choose with safety in mind. Skateboarding can be dangerous, but it doesn't have to be. Quite often it's a matter of good sense.

It makes good sense to take someone along with you who is already into the sport. There is no teacher like experience. Someone, who has taken a bad spill because of faulty equipment, has learned the hard way about boards, trucks (units that wheels are mounted on) and wheels. The cheapest board may not be the safest board. However, the board with the highest price tag may be more than you need as a beginner. You may want another board when you become an expert at one kind of skating such as racing, trick skating, or slalom.

Whether you choose a skateboard made of wood, fiberglass or aluminum, choose the middle of the price range. As you develop your own style, you may decide you need several boards for different purposes. You may also decide to make your own after you learn about boards, wheels, and truck assemblies.

11

Now you have a skateboard. However, that isn't the end of the safety story. You must be prepared for those spills you're going to take. It's foolish not to protect yourself. Wear a helmet, elbow pads, knee pads, gloves, and good shoes. Then you can take those spills in stride. You won't be sidelined with injuries. (Wearing these things will also keep your parents happy!)

Ready for your first ride? Here goes! Check over the area carefully. Your own driveway or an empty parking lot is a good place to begin. Be sure it has a clean surface. Loose stones or sticks may cause you to fall even before you get a chance to try anything fancy! The surface should also be dry. Skating through puddles just after a rain may sound like great fun, but any experienced skater will tell you that water and wheels don't mix — especially if those wheels are urethane! It's the fastest fall there is!

STAN SHARP

13

Now, climb aboard. Stand with your feet at an angle on the board. Most people stand with the left foot in front. Some feel more natural with the right foot forward. This is called goofy-foot, but if it feels right for you, it isn't goofy!

Position the feet.

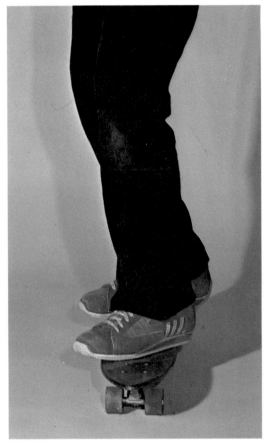

Left foot forward.

Right foot forward.

Bend your knees just a little. Use your arms for balance. Push off with your back foot. If you are taking your first ride on a flat surface, you will have to lean forward a little to go forward. If you are on a slight incline, gravity will take you forward. But, be sure it's a slight incline. You don't want to tempt gravity on your first ride! You also want to be sure it levels off so you can stop. You're not an expert - yet!

Push off!

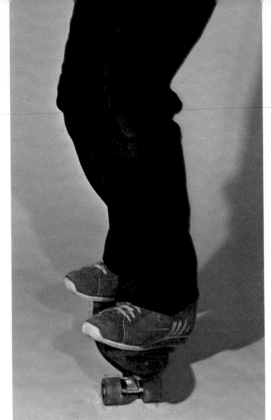 

Left turn position.   *Right turn position.*

Lean toward the direction you want to go. The wheels under you will listen. They will go in the direction your body weight tells them. Suddenly, you are in command. You can turn! If you wobble a little, be patient. You'll get over the wobbles with practice.

Next, you are ready for some basic moves. Skateboarding is so much like surfing that some of the moves have the same names. Wiping out on concrete is different from wiping out on water. Each has its own dangers; learn to take a fall, get up, and try again!

Ready to hang ten? Let's go. Put your feet close together with all ten toes hanging over the end of the board. You must balance the board with your heels so the back of the board stays on the ground. If you don't you might take a nose dive!

Maybe you have seen skaters riding their boards in a sitting position. Try it. It really isn't sitting since you don't sit on the board. It's called the crouch.

Put both feet on the center of the board facing forward. Bend your knees all the way. Push off with your hands, and stretch your arms out in front of you for balance.

Ed Nadalin hangs ten!

To avoid "hamburger toes" we suggest you wear shoes.

Everybody who ever had a skateboard wants to do a wheelie. When you feel comfortable on your board, you will want to try it. Here's how. By now you know that the front of your board is its nose and the back is its tail. To do a nose wheelie, put your feet on the board as you did to hang ten. Then move your feet back just enough so that the soles of your feet are directly over the front wheels. Bend your knees a little, stretch out your arms and feel the tail of the board rise. Ride like this and you are doing a nose wheelie!

To do a tail wheelie, place the soles of your feet directly over the rear wheels. Bend your knees and press backward with your heels to lift the front of the board. You still have to lean forward a little for balance. Now you're doing a tail wheelie!

The kick-turn is a move you'll want to learn. It looks like a move for experts, but after you have practiced your basic moves and feel confident, you will want to try it. Push down on the tail behind the wheels. At the same time, lift the front foot. The front wheels will leave the ground. Now you can kick the board to either side. That's a snappy-looking kick-turn, and it is fun! You'll have so much fun doing this move that you will practice it often. In no time you will become a kick-turn expert.

STAN SHARP

19

THE "KICK-TURN"

At this time you will probably feel ready for 180's and even 360's. A 180 is nothing but a kick-turn that faces you in the opposite direction from where you started. Just stay with the kick-turn until you are facing the other direction. Stay in it until you are back where you started from, and you have done a 360! Sound easy? It's just like everything else you have ever tried to do. The first tries may be so clumsy that you will wonder how anyone ever does it. Then you will begin to get the feel of it and you're there. And you got there the same way the violinist got to Carnegie Hall — practice! Don't give up. Think of the fun you had learning all your basic moves. They didn't all come out right the first time either, did they?

"Nice wheelie."

STAN SHARP

22

These are only a few of the moves you can learn on your skateboard. The more you skate, the more confident you will become. You will try new moves. Maybe you will begin to look like some of the experts. They all started the same way you did — one step at a time.

Sooner or later you will probably begin to think about competition. These contests have become very important in cities where skateboarding is popular. There are national contests with big prize money. There is even talk about putting skateboarding in the Olympic contests. In September, 1977, the world championship prize money was more than $20,000.

A few cones and a slanted sidewalk are all you need to start practicing.

When a skater enters a contest, he has already begun to be expert in a certain kind of skating. There are racing competitions, trick-riding, freestyle, and slalom. Most of these contests are sponsored by the big manufacturers of skateboards. They organize teams for team competition. The company pays all the expenses for the team members. If the team wins the contest, it's good advertisement for the skateboard company. The best skaters in the country compete to be on these teams which makes the competition very keen. Some skaters make up new tricks of their own to impress the judges. The company rules usually require safety equipment. They don't want to lose any of their top skaters! They also want to promote safe skating.

A tricky skateboard pyramid.

"Three to go, hold on man."

STAN SHARP

You might want to organize your own neighborhood competition. Get together with some of your skating pals and decide on a place to hold your contest. A parent, teacher, or local businessperson could be helpful to you in getting permission to hold the contest. Decide on a date and time, select judges, find sponsors to donate prizes or trophies, advertise, and go to it. Who knows? Someone may do something so super in winning your local contest that he or she could attract national attention, and be invited to compete in one of the big contests. It could be you!

If you would like information about skateboards and skateboard contests, you may write to either of the following organizations:

Pacific Skateboard Association
P.O. Box 2025
Leucadia, CA. 92629

Pro-Am Skateboard Racing Association
P.O. Box 578
Dana Point, CA. 92629

"The crowd loves it."

STAN SHARP

*"Just over" in
the high-jumping
competition.*

If there is a skateboard park or arena in your town, they may be sponsoring contests. There will probably be an entry fee which goes to pay for the prizes. Some of these contests are fun to watch, even if you're not ready to be a contestant.

Besides the racing, trick-riding, and freestyle contests, there occasionally are contests in barrel-jumping and high-jumping. These are dangerous tricks, so don't try them until you have a lot of experience!

The people jump.

No matter what kind of skating you do, the most important thing to remember is safety. It may look "cool" to grab that skateboard and go, without bothering to use your safety equipment. In fact, you will be tempted to do just that after you have some experience with your board. Keep in mind there is concrete under you. Broken bones and "hamburger toes" are not cool. They can rob you of your fun for a long time. So play it safe! Stay with your good sense approach to skating.

Another thing you will want to keep in mind, as you become more daring with your skateboard, is to obey the laws of your town. Officials in some cities have a bad opinion of skateboarders because of the foolishness of a few. If skateboard regulations have been set for your community, make it your business to know and obey them. If there are none, let common sense be your guide. It's just common courtesy not to use sidewalks that must be used by shoppers carrying packages, mothers strolling their babies, and older people walking. Help give skateboarding a good name by being considerate of other people.

Skateboarding is great fun and good exercise. Go out and have a good time on your wheels.

Riding the tube.

STAN SHARP

STAN SHARP